Dismantled

Christian Poetry

David LaChapelle

⁶ being confident of this, that he who began a good work in you will carry it on to completion until the day of Christ Jesus.

Philippians 1:6 (NIV)

ISBN: 9798313535128

Independently Published

POEMS

24 I tell you the truth, unless a kernel of wheat is planted in the soil and dies, it remains alone. But its death will produce many new kernels—a plentiful harvest of new lives.

John 12:24 (NLT)

Rising

Pushed into the ground

Wearing a frown

Rebel retaliation

Natural Salutation

Reach the top

To see the score

To have some power to overthrow

Given a crutch

To settle me down

So, I do not hurt myself

And be raised by Him alone

<u>All</u>

Thorn in the flesh

To disturb my rest

To keep me on my toes

So many foes

Cannot trust my own

Flowing down the river

Streams in the desert

To quench the thirst

To a parched and dry course

All I have is Him

He makes me win

More

Out of supply

Water to wine is fine

Performing to get good

The desire to be obedient

Seems so gradient

Wanting nothing but Him

To please in all aspects

To trust my heart

And do my part

Believing in something more

Then keeping score

Acceptance

I apologize

For the way I behaved

For what I did not believe

Am a human being

Cannot come to a conclusion

No more delusion

No way to win

Just accept Him

Working within

Bide my time

Blooming in the skies

Everything is fine

Ceasing

Lost in you

Nothing to unglue

Less of me

More to see

Accepted in the beloved

Belonging to Him

Forevermore

Not afraid to face the score

Not afraid to face the judgment

My heart is well spoken

I want to do the best

He will do the rest

Being

Cannot live up to false ideals

Come to terms

That God is real

Nothing to prove

Nothing to lose

Feel the love

In the beloved

Like I belong

In a holy song

Not trying to break free

Chains removed

I can be

<u>Beginning</u>

Trying to do things on my own

Left a bad taste in my soul

Hurt and pain invade

That was the game played

Felt like I had to win

To gain more of Him

Losing my life for Christ did the opposite

So, suffice

Try not to think twice

Now I have freedom

To be the man

Who believes in Him

Sin no longer dominates

I can begin

To relate to others where they are

Is what this is all for

Grace wins every time

No matter the crime

Rebel felony against

Born with a fallen nature

Adam and Eve

The start of creation

Elation and celebration

Breaking

Trying to earn God's favor

Left a bad flavor

Not knowing what I was doing

Hurtful to me so soon

Unconscious in the scheme

Cycle kept repeating

Had to be broken

This final time

To give up my will

And not to be benign

Fighting Him

All the way to the bank

Fearing the consequences

I sank

Being vulnerable

Was a fantasy

Made so real

Playing defence

Deceptive ego

Validate its existence

An illusive phantom of care

Till I realized

His love is for real

Set free

A new deal to steal

He Won

Fighting condemnation

Draining my resources

No more sources

Bound by the struggle

Taken captive

By my will

No thrill

So still

A prisoner with a window

Hope on the scene

He would not let me go

To my own devices

Anything other than His love

Seemed good to me

What I thought I really need

Thought I could save myself

Self preservation

Deceived by sin

Rebelling His love

God is greater

Master chess game player

Checkmate

I found favor

Witness

My supply came to an end

He took over again

I am a witness

To see how He works

No longer blinded by a foggy heart

Pain clouded my thinking

Pain clouded my feeling

I was dying to myself and hurt

Now a new start

I am all His

Seeing the love of Christ

In my daily life

No longer blindsided

I am confided

Knowing Him

Is the way to begin

Easier to trust now

He has revealed Himself to me

I do not doubt like I would

Even in the toughest times

I see him as good and in charge

Undone

Grace is Grace

Without the help of me

I bring nothing to table

Let's have dinner

To earn his favor

Everyone is a winner

Trying to break free

Was limiting me

His love is enough

For all my stuff

What a sight to see

Beautiful to be undone

The Lord has rescued me

He did all the work

Knowing Him

I feel loved

From above

Casting

I cannot do anything

Out of His sight

He knows better than my might

I have nothing to offer

Nothing in the coffers

Opening my arms

To discover

His work manifesting in my life

He works through circumstances

And His creations flowing to frequency

His evidence all over the place

Nothing to be hindered or opposed

I am all His

Hallelujah!

He has my vote

<u>Free</u>

Mellow fellow

Resting in peace

Not divided

Focus clarified

I am all His

It is a nice feeling

To keep on believing

In something greater than me

He will show me the day

Do not want my own way

Floating in liberty

Is the sweetest sound

I am free

New Start

Self effort

Is not wasted time

Coming to the line

Bound by the climb

Living in denial

Is a trial

Come to terms again

That I am not well within

Need a new deal

Not to steal

His love from above

Is a new start

Fresh from the heart

Is what it is all about

No more clout

No more pout

Opened Up

Through the fire

No time to tire

Brought to the end

A new beginning

Pressure squeezed out what was hiding

Holding onto fear of death

Emptying me out of me

Nothing left

Fell off the cliff

I now see

He caught me

My true feelings

Opened up to the ceilings

<u>End</u>

The last straw

Nothing to draw

Sword knocked down

No more frown

Please Him in all respects

Squeezed out

No more pout

No more doubt

I am all His

That is what life is supposed to be

In the scheme of things

That is what rings

True to His Word

He is the Lord

<u>Returning</u>

Hidden pain

Brought to the light of day

No more strain

Broken in two

Come unglued

Made whole

In my soul

Squeezed fruit

No more toot

Complacency to have my way

No more stray

I am here to stay

In your arms forevermore

The door is open

I am all yours

Receiving

All His

Nothing to stress

He has all of me

I am comforted

With not knowing

What will eventually be

Freedom is found

When I do not make a sound

Clamoring noise to displease

Harmony inside

Where I am open to find

His love waiting on me

Wow!

Chastened

Faced death

No more breath

Backed into a corner

Nothing to shoulder

Surrender to His love

Saw who I really am

Squeezed out for the last time

Under pressure

No more stressor

More peace

Made whole

After the storm

Lost control

Nowhere to go

Only to Him

And, His loving open arms

Forevermore

Pleased

Broken whole

Freedom in my soul

No more need for control

Nothing to prove

Now I can groove

To my hearts content

No thorn in the flesh

Your love never relents

You broke down the fence

What I was holding onto

And revealed my real opinion of you

Repressed anger released

I am no longer depressed

I am pleased

Trophy

Molded like clay

A trophy of His Grace

Evident for all to see

His love in me

Had to be a broken seed

A fragrance of peace

Calm the storm inside

To settle down the world and pride

Called where I am

A servant of Jesus

Cannot be explained away

In the fray

Of everyday

Journey

No running away

I am in your arms to stay

In your love forevermore

Keeping score, no more

Freedom found

Chains broken down

Feel whole and complete

What a journey and feat

To get to this place

Through such intense heat

Follow His lead

Without begging for need

Cooled off

Stay the course

Is not an obligation

It is revelation

It is celebration

Elaborating me to be me

Ready

I am motivated to please

The one who created me

Not my own desires that count

His blessings are a fountain of love

Peace and harmony, does not elude

It is permanent

Do not have to worry about my temperament

My emotions are stable

The war is over

No more fable

I am at the table

Ready for supper

With Him for eternity

What a sight to see

In Need

Agitation and frustration, has left me

No more struggle

Looking over my trouble

I am content and at peace

Ever since I had fears

From the beginning of my tears

That plagued me

Bringing me to my knees

Pleading please

Have mercy Lord

I am in need

Love me

Motivation

I am motivated

To continue

This over rated

Life on this stage

Playing my part

Is a start

To bring me to my knees

Brought down low

To put on a show

For everyone to see

When He raises me

Above the scene

For His glory

And my victory

So, we can be free

Speaking in His love

Come back to me

Pride

Pushed to the ground
Did not make a sound
Just complained
In my wicked complacency
That I am enough
To handle this rough
Was a lie I could not fully believe
Locked in His grace
I was able to face
The war within me
To be in control
And know more than my soul
Was never going to be
Now on the right side
Of His being

I am free with glee

Testimony

No worry

No hurry

No flurry of emotions

Or fury haunting my soul

Under pressure

Released from the dresser

What I was holding onto

Driving the colors of my life

And the lens I viewed the world

To be renewed

A fresh start

From the heart

Is my testimony

Nothing needs to be said

I can be read

To let it all out

And be found

Shouting how much He loves us

Relating

The cares of this life
Has passed me by this time
No need to worry
He is in control
No need to hurry
He loves my soul
Whatever will be will be
I cannot change reality
To make it suit me
I am free
To rest in His presence
And not falter beyond measure
That I am all His
Filled with peace
It is my pleasure to believe

To surrender
To His loving Grace
I can now relate

Delivered

The cares of this life

Has passed me by

I will do what needs to be

Cannot do anything more

To reorder the store

What He has delivered for me

Resting in peace

Reality is pure

When your perspective is sure

Loving kindness

I await your answer

To my prayers

Nothing more to see

I trust you Lord

Nothing can separate

You are in control

What better place to be

Counting no more

Loving the score

In His arms

Forevermore

Care

I do not carry care

Jesus knows more than me

The Lord will do what He can

He will show me the place

What success is supposed to be

Not doubt His love

Not doubt His provision

Jesus knows what is the best decision

In every season

I can attest

And rest

That wrestling with fears

Only brings tears

I am trusting the Lord now

He will tell me how

To be the best in every scene
To please Him and His love be seen

Full

I am out the door

Nothing to store

Not living in regret

Not harboring animosity

Owing no one condolences

For my lack I once had

I can give out and not receive

Correcting the I pain I once had

Now I am glad

And free to love

The stars above

Healing societies plead

Only way to win over sin

Restoration is redeemed

He won the chess game

Bringing me to my knees

I am all His now

Nothing to tow

A lighter load

Better flow

Peace does not evade

I can now be free to be who I am meant to be

Apology

I have been forgiven

From being driven

Into ground

So much sound

Of condemnation and shame

Guilt too please

Nothing to prove

Nothing to lose

Just my pride

A thorn in my side

Regulating me

Trying to hide

My true feelings inside

Did not want to offend

Could not be the man

I wanted to be

Now I am free

The storm settled down

I am wearing a crown

No more dark

That is all I can see

Convinced

It is all new to me

To proclaim the good news so freely

I feel like a loon

A dollar coin so soon

Going into the vending machine

Purchasing a drink

To quench my thirsty brink

His currency is all I need

Help me stay the course

And not try to force

His love for me

Do not want to be proud

Do not want to be loud

Forgive me for being so bold

I am sold on Jesus alone

Leashed

Wanted to fight

Deep into the night

To have my own way

He would not let me go

The pain was not you

Not knowing I was the fool

Now you have my soul

I can see

Deceptive ego

Seems subsided

For the time being

Surrendering to your love

Is an ongoing process

For all those involved

The case is solved

Endless

Time will tell

How deep is the well

His love for me

Drawing out life

In the heat of the night

Like a summer's eve

Refreshed by the ocean waves

There is nothing undue

My spirit has been renewed

The debt has been paid

Purchased the ransom for the lost

And all that come to Him

Do not delay

There may not be another day

To settle the score

This is what redemption is for

Eternity

Forevermore

Surrender

Resisting your love

Is not from above

Born rebellion was all me

Brought the end of pleading

Nothing to win

Quiet victory

I belong to Jesus

No more sin within

Focusing on His love

For all those involved

Thank God

I am alive

During these last days

Come what may

ABOUT THE AUTHOR

David LaChapelle is a born-again Christian since the year 2000. David has earned himself two Computer Technical Diplomas from Seneca College, in Toronto, Canada in 1994 and 1996. He graduated with a Psychology degree in 2011, from Trent University in Peterborough, Canada, where he now calls home. David lives a quiet life and enjoys writing and being an author. He is proud of his works, and hopes it will bring him recognition in this life and rewards hereafter. David is a firm believer in reading the Word of God, and the power of prayer and wishes the best for all humanity awaiting the Lord's return.

OTHER BOOKS BY DAVID LACHAPELLE

David's Adventure with Schizophrenia: My Road to Recovery

David's Journey with Schizophrenia: Insight into Recovery

David's Victory Thru Schizophrenia: Healing Awareness

David's Poems: A Poetry Collection

1000 Canadian Expressions and Meanings: EH!

David's Faith Poems: Christian Poetry

Freedom in Jesus

Canadian Slang Sayings and Meanings: Eh!

The Biggest Collection of Canadian Slang: Eh!

Healing Hidden Emotions for Believers

Breaking Clouds: Christian Poetry

Walking Light: Christian Poetry

Let Go: Christian Poetry

David's Faith Poems II: Christian Poetry

Eternity Calling: Christian Poetry

Receiving Grace: Christian Poetry

Humbled: Mental Health, Addiction and Christian Poetry

All books and e-books available at Amazon